Fearless and confident, Paris elegantly balances a forward thinking mentality ... ways one step ... set- ting the s ... ood, music an ... ng-e side quin ... dge cuisine, \ ... g night sce

CITIx60: Paris explores the French capital in five aspects, covering architecture, art spaces, shops and markets, eating and entertainments. With expert advice from 60 stars of Paris' creative scene, this book guides you to the real attractions of the city for an authentic taste of Paris life.

Contents

Before You Go

BASIC INFO

Currency
Euro (EUR/€)
Exchange rate: €1 : $1.16

Time zone
GMT +1
DST +2

DST begins at 0200 (local time) on the last Sunday in March and ends at 0300 (local time) on the last Sunday in October.

Dialling
International calling: +33
Citywide: 01

Weather (avg. temperature range)
Spring (Apr–Jun): 9–20°C / 48–68°F
Summer (Jul–Aug): 15–25°C / 59–77°F
Autumn (Oct–Dec): 5–13°C / 41–55°F
Winter (Jan–Mar): 1–12°C / 34–54°F

USEFUL WEBSITES

Citywide public transport networks
www.ratp.fr/tourists

Regional train ticket reservations & status
www.sncf.com

EMERGENCY CALLS

Ambulance (SAMU) / Fire
15 / 18

Police
17

Embassies / consulates
China   +33 (0)1 49 52 19 50
Japan   +33 (0)1 48 88 62 00
Germany   +33 (0)1 53 83 45 00
UK   +33 (0)1 44 51 31 00
US   +33 (0)1 43 12 22 22

AIRPORT EXPRESS TRANSFER

Aéroport CDG T2 <–> Châtelet Les Halles (RER B)
Trains / Journey: every 10–20min / 25–30min
From Charles de Gaulle Airport – 0450-2350
From Châtelet Les Halles – 0519-0046
One-way: €11.40/7.90

Aéroport Orly <–> Antony <–> Châtelet Les Halles
Orlyval / Journey: every 5–7min / 8min
From Orly-Sud/Antony – 0600-2335
RER B / Journey: every 10–15min / 20–25min
From Antony – 0508-2351
From Châtelet Les Halles – 0523-2226
One-way: €12.10/6.05

www.aeroportsdeparis.fr

PUBLIC TRANSPORT IN PARIS

Metro
Train (RER & SNCF)
Boat
Bus
Taxi
Vélib'

Means of Payment
Credit card (Metro ticket window)
Cash

PUBLIC HOLIDAYS

January	1 New Year's Day
March/April	Easter Monday
May	1 Labour Day, 8 Victory 1945, Ascension Day, Whit Monday
July	14 Bastille Day
August	15 Assumption Day
November	1 All Saints' Day, 11 Armistice 1918
December	25 Christmas Day

Museums, galleries and shops are likely to be closed on Jan 1, May 1 and/or Dec 25, or have varied opening hours on public holidays.

FESTIVALS / EVENTS

January
Paris Fashion Week: Men (also in June), Haute
Couture (also in July)
fhcm.paris
Maison & Objet (Also in September)
www.maison-objet.com/en

February
Paris Fashion Week: Women (Also in September)
fhcm.paris
Première Vision (Also in September)
www.premierevision.com

April
Art Paris
www.artparis.com/en

May
Des Ateliers d'Artistes de Belleville Open House
ateliers-artistes-belleville.fr/en
Cannes Best – Directors' Fortnight
(through to June)
www.quinzaine-realisateurs.com

August
Rock en Seine
www.rockenseine.com
Jazz à la Villette (through to September)
www.jazzalavillette.com

September
Paris Design Week
www.maison-objet.com/en/paris-design-week

October
International Contemporary Art Fair (FIAC)
www.fiac.com
Nuit Blanche
quefaire.paris.fr/nuitblanche

November
Offprint Paris – Art Publishing Fair
offprint.org

Event days vary by year. Please check for
updates online.

UNUSUAL OUTINGS

Bluefox Travel
www.bluefox.travel/paris

GA Tour
www.ga-paris.fr

Paris by Martin
parisbymartin.com

Paris Muse
www.parismuse.com

Treasure Hunt at the Museum
www.thatmuse.com

Street Art Paris
streetartparis.fr

SMARTPHONE APP

Weekly gig guide & exhibition highlights
DOJO: City Discovery

Bike routes, locator & available bikes/docks
Vélib'

Self-service electric mopeds (age 18+)
Cityscoot

Latest news reports on France & Paris
FRANCE 24

REGULAR EXPENSES

Expresso
€1.80–2.80

Domestic / EU / International mails
€0.73 / 1.10 / 1.30

Gratuities
Diners: 5–10% for waitstaff & bartenders
Hotels: €1@bag for the porter, €2 daily for
cleaners
Licensed taxis: 5–10%

Count to 10

What makes Paris so special?
Illustrations by Guillaume Kashima aka Funny Fun

The beauty of this city originates in the people's love for simple pleasure, freedom and life. From a morning coffee to late-night concert, Paris is where you can take things easy, and revel with all your senses. Don't fuss. Don't rush. Whether you are on a one-day stopover or a week-long stay, see what Paris creatives consider essential to see, taste, read and take home from your trip.

1

Museums & Cultural Centres

Centre Pompidou (#13)
www.centrepompidou.fr

Muséum National d'Histoire Naturelle
www.mnhn.fr

Institut du Monde Arabe
www.imarabe.org

Musée du quai Branly
www.quaibranly.fr

Maison Européenne de la Photographie
www.mep-fr.org

Le Comptoir Général (#58)
www.lecomptoirgeneral.com

5

Wine & Cheese

Bourgogne wine
Marsannay or Hautes Côtes de
Nuit (Robert Jayer-Gilles)
La Crèmerie
FB: @lacremerieparis

(Ask Sylvain Thieblemont)
Le Vin en Tête
www.levinentete.fr

Cheese
Fromagerie Quatrehomme
www.quatrehomme.fr

Fontainebleau
La Ferme Saint-Hubert
www.la-ferme-saint-hubert-de-
paris.com

Laurent Dubois
www.fromageslaurentdubois.fr

6

Concerts &
Live Gigs

Petit Bain
www.petitbain.org

Le Batofar
www.batofar.fr

Point Éphémère (#17)
www.pointephemere.org

**Cité de la Musique –
Philharmonie de Paris**
philharmoniedeparis.fr

7

Leisure

**Get lost & make
discoveries on the streets**
16th arr.

Picnic
Canal Saint Martin (#2)
or along the Seine River

**Play ping-pong & pétanque by
Canal de l'Ourcq**
BarOurcq
68 quai de la Loire,
La Villette, 75019

**Watch a movie outdoor
in summer**
Cinéma au Clair de Lune
or Cinéma en Plein Air

Breakfast at Les Deux Abeilles
189 r. de l'Université, 75007

8

Mementos

A Gainsbourg record
Porte de Vanves Flea Market

Nadja by André Breton
Surrealist romance originally
published in 1928

**A cool T-shirt from
Kitsuné's "Parisien" Collection**
Maison Kitsuné
kitsune.fr

Vintage improbable objects
Tombées du Camion
17 r. Joseph de Maistre, 75018
www.tombeesducamion.com

Serge Lutens perfume
Palais Royal – Serge Lutens
www.sergelutens.com

9

Trace Of Legends

Maison de Victor Hugo
www.maisonsvictorhugo.paris.fr

Musée Gustave-Moreau
www.musee-moreau.fr

Maison de Serge Gainsbourg
5bis r. Verneuil,
Saint Thomas d'Aquin, 75007

Père-Lachaise Cemetery (#6)
Tombs of revered artists,
novelists & politicians

Café de la Rotonde
Long established hotspot for
writers and painters
105 blvd. du Montparnasse, 75006

**Coco Chanel's
apartment & shop**
*31 r. Cambon, Place Vendôme,
75001*

10

Scenes In
French Movies

Louvre galleries
Bande à Part (1964)
by Jean-Luc Godard

**Canal Saint-Martin (#2),
Café des 2 Moulins**
Amélie (2001)
by Jean-Pierre Jeunet

Avenue des Champs Elysée
À bout de souffle (1960)
by Jean-Luc Godard

Le Sacré Coeur
Les quatre cents coups (1959)
by François Truffaut

La Samaritaine
Holy Motors (2012)
by Leos Carax

La Pont-Neuf
Les Amants du Pont-Neuf (1991)
by Leos Carax

Icon Index

 Opening hours   Admission

 Address   Facebook

Contact   Website

Remarks

 Scan QR codes to access Google Maps and discover the area around each destination. Internet connection required.

60x60

60 Local Creatives x 60 Hotspots

From vast cityscapes to the smallest snippets of conversation, there is much to inspire creative urges in Paris. 60x60 points you to 60 haunts where 60 arbiters of taste develop their nose for the good stuff.

Landmarks & Architecture
SPOTS · 01 – 12

Paris fuses classics and contemporary spaces to give it a unique and picturesque cityscape. The métro, city bikes or Paris' streets are each a perfect guide through the city.

Cultural & Art Spaces
SPOTS · 13 – 24

Besides painting and sculpture, Paris' museums celebrate nature and the city's history. Indulge in the building designs as much as the diverse collections they hold.

Markets & Shops
SPOTS · 25 – 36

Fine art auctions, local produce, vintage fashion and rare art books all go to show a Parisian's aptitude for life and culture beyond avenue des Champs-Élysées.

Restaurants & Cafés
SPOTS · 37 – 48

Pastries, cheese and wines are still what you're after although neo-French culinary are on the rise. Eat without worry as rarely you can spot overweight Parisians on the street.

Nightlife
SPOTS · 49 – 60

Play hard in Paris – whether you crave recitals, techno, jazz, cinema. Rowdy pubs or highbrow arts in Paris put on every kind of show. Bring a picnic for concerts in the parks!

Landmarks & Architecture

Modernist architecture, cultural establishments and majestic parks

Cities don't come as perfectly balanced as Paris. A blend of neo-classical architecture, experimental glass structures and vast green spaces punctuate the capital, whilst an equally diverse set of characters pulse through its veins.

Rich with a history both complex and legendary, remnant structures from the 17th and 18th century retain astonishing authority and influence, with alignment and frequent uniformity of height being a recognisable trait that characterises the city's narrow, interweaving streets. Architectural initiatives inside Paris have been constrained since the 1600s with strict regulations regarding height and shape. Flagship icons such as the Eiffel Tower (#4) and Notre Dame on the Île de la Cité are indeed unquestionable destinations for any visitor, as are the majestic Arab World Institute (*1 r. Fossés Saint-Bernard, Saint-Victor, 75005*) and gleaming skyscrapers clustered in La Defense. Nevertheless, make it a priority to also explore the cult areas currently attracting alternative, trendy crowds. Admire the modernist glass lustre of La Maison de Verre (*31 r. Saint-Guillaume, Saint-Thomas d'Aquin, 75007*), for instance, and stroll across the vast range of parks which offer strong modern and historic design features – Jardin des Tuileries hosts a beautiful French garden dotted with hexagonal ponds and stunning statues, perfect for a summer picnic. Whether travelling by bike, boat or foot, Paris is famed for its leisurely pace – take a stroll and let the city lead you to its wonders.

Baptiste Rouget-Luchaire, *Film director*

I make documentary films which allows me to travel a lot but I'm always happy to come back to my city. I hope you will like this city. Paris is a city of good surprises.

Canal Saint-Martin 015

MWM Graphics
Graphic artist

I'm originally from Boston, currently living in Paris. I divide my time between digital illustration, painting massive murals, and doing fine art exhibitions in galleries.

STUDIO PLASTAC
Graphic designer

Plastac runs both self initiated projects and commissions on screen, paper and in volume. We specially stand out in the areas of graphic identities, publishing and animation.

Place des Vosges 014

Iris de Moüy
Illustrator

Born and based in Paris. I author children's books and draw for magazines like ELLE and brands like Hermès, Air France and Le Bon Marché. I love Paris!

Grande Mosquée de Paris 018

Chloé Desvenain
Graphic designer

I'm a 27-year old freelance graphic designer also known as Fakepaper. I love my work because it allows me to meet new people and keeps me moving forward.

Jérémy Murier
Product designer

I principally create fashion accessories like watches and eyewear for a French brand and myself as a freelancer. I've completed studies in Paris, Marseille, and Lausanne.

Les Docks 016

Tour Eiffel 017

Cimetière du Père-Lachaise 020

Leslie Dubest
Artists & repertoire

I'm 39, French, A&R, creative director and a dad of two. I love music foremost and arts overall. I've been in the music business since 20 and co-founded The:Hours (now Forward).

Hôtel National des Invalides 022

Patrick Norguet
Industrial & interior designer

A free spirit consistently in search of "the right line." My focus is interior architecture projects, for important publishers like Cassina, Alias, and Cappellini.

Sophie Gateau
Film director

I began my career creating live action films for runways. I've since been a commercial and music video director, and was graphic artist for *The Matrix Reloaded* (2003) and *2046* (2004).

Jardin du Luxembourg 021

Parc des Buttes-Chaumont 023

Julie Rothhahn
Food designer

I apprehend food from a designer's point of view. I shape it, direct it, set it up and try to give it a meaning, which then becomes sensitive, regressive or even transgressive.

Siège du PCF, Espace Niemeyer 025

Sophie Toporkoff
Art director

I've been the Communication Art Director of Maison Martin Margiela, created magazines and drawn a lot. I'm ever in search of new ideas or impulse through my work.

Manuelle Gautrand
Architect

I'm a French architect, and I founded MANUELLE GAUTRAND ARCHITECTURE in 1991. You will find several of my buildings in Paris, including Barclay Headquarters in the 8th arr.

Villa Savoye 024

Citroën C42 026

1 Place des Vosges
Map H, P.108

Thirty-six symmetrical red brick and stone houses square off an elegant plot of land in the Marais district. In fact, this tasteful landmark is the oldest square in Paris and a listed historic monument since 1954. An arcade with art galleries, shops, hotels and cafés on its perimeter, Place des Vosges was home to Victor Hugo, author of *Les Miserable* and *Notre-Dame de Paris* (1831), who lived at No.6. To get a formal taste of Parisian architecture, stroll around the site's four corners before perching next to one of its grand fountains.

🏠 Arsenal, 75004
🔗 Maison de Victor Hugo: 1000-1800 (Tu-Su), maisonsvictorhugo.paris.fr

"The most beautiful square in Paris. Picnic in the garden."
– Baptiste Rouget-Luchaire

2 Canal Saint–Martin

Map G, P.107

Connecting the Seine and Bassin de la Villette, Canal Saint–Martin was opened as a 4.5km shipping link between the city and the suburbs in 1825 and is now a magnet for bourgeois Parisian bohemians. With nine locks, two swing bridges and vaulted tunnels where the waterway runs underground, its picturesque scenery offers a perfect backdrop for picnics during the day and drinks with friends at night. Eye up the characters that mill along the canal's path, which leads up to Point Éphémère (#17). Du Pain et Des Idées at 34 rue Yves Toudic is one boulangerie you should not miss.

🏠 *Porte Saint–Martin, 75010*

"On a nice day, walk from République east along the canal for an hour through interesting neighbourhoods filled with graffiti and street-level culture."

– MWM Graphics

3 Les Docks –
Cité de la mode et du design

Map N, P.111

With exposed exterior walls and a new giant glass rooftop, the 1907 concrete warehouse revived by architects Dominique Jakob and Brenda MacFarlane in 1998 is now a meeting point for artisans and brands, and home to l'Institut Français de la Mode. Trawl through the many galleries and designer shops across the 20,000sqm hub, grab lunch at meat-free fast food joint M.O.B and party hard at the legendary Wanderlust or Nuba (#51). For a complete view of the structure and the caterpillar-like top dipping along the Seine, make your entrance through Gare de Lyon.

🕐 1000–0000 daily
🏠 34 quai d'Austerlitz, Salpêtrière, 75013
☎ +33 (0)1 7677 2530
URL www.citemodedesign.fr

"It's an amazing futuristic architecture along the Seine. Enjoy the view on the rooftop."
– STUDIO PLASTAC

4   Tour Eiffel
Map L, P.111

Built by Gustave Eiffel (1835–1923) for the 1889 Exposition Universelle that celebrated the French Revolution's centenary, the Eiffel Tower is the quintessential emblem of Paris. At a staggering 324 metres, the 19th century iron structure was a milestone in French engineering, once the world's tallest building and now an essential reference when speaking about the city's romance. Famous for providing unrivalled views of the capital, nothing says Paris more than sipping champagne at the top of the tower whilst peering over the Louvre and Notre Dame lit up against the night sky.

🕐 *0900–0045 daily, Easter weekend & spring holidays, 0930–2345 (Sep 2–Jun 14)*
💲 *€17/14.50/11/8.50* 🏠 *5 av. Anatole France, Gros Caillou, 75007* 🔗 *www.toureiffel.paris*
✏ *Last admission: 45 min before closing*

"Because it is magical at night! Read my book, En route pour la tour Eiffel, and you will know how to find it!"

– Iris de Moüy

5 Grande Mosquée de Paris
Map I, P.109

Situated in the heart of Paris, this teal-roofed structure is the city's largest mosque, and the third largest in Europe. Completed in 1926 to honour the North African countries that aided France during World War I, the Hispano-Moor-esque style building is decked with intricate detailing, from sweeping marble floors to vibrant tiling and exquisite water features. If curiosity gets the better of you, take a guided tour for historical insights into the Islamic faith, or lounge on the lush cushions in the mosque's café and tea room with some aromatic sweets.

🕙 0900-1200, 1400-1800 (Sa-Th, except Muslim holidays), summer: -1900 💲 €3
🏠 2bis Pl. Puits de l'Ermite, Jardin des Plantes, 75005 📞 +33 (0)1 4535 9733
🔗 www.mosqueedeparis.net
🎫 Guided tours: 0900, 1200, 1400, 1800

"Go at 5pm, sit on the terrace, and take pastry with a mint tea. Then watch sparrows dancing around eating your cake crumbs."

– Chloé Desvenain aka Fakepaper

6　Cimetière du Père-Lachaise
Map P, P.111

Named after Louis XIV's confessor, Père Lachaise Cemetery was a serene Jesuit retreat until Napoleon declared it an equitable burial ground in 1804. Being the largest urban grave-yard in Paris, the tree-filled site is also home to such luminous figures as Frédéric Chopin, Jim Morrison, Edith Piaf, and Oscar Wilde – all marked by memorials and ornate stones. Exit at Philippe Auguste (M2) station to access the main entrance. The Cemetery office offers free maps at 16 rue du Repos.

🕐 0800–1800 (M–F), 0830– (Sa), 0900– (Su & P.H.), –1730 daily (Nov 6–Mar 15)　🚏 8 blvd. Menilmontant, Père-Lachaise, 75020
📞 +33 (0)1 5525 8210　🔗 equipement.paris.fr/cimetiere-du-pere-lachaise-4080

"A very interesting and quaint site to visit. Its organisation, built like a micro-city with family vault for the oldest part, is original and disturbing!"
– Jérémy Murier

7 Jardin du Luxembourg

Map M, P.111

Between the university zone "Quartier Latin" and Montparnasse lies the Luxembourg Gardens, the second largest public park in Paris and the garden of the Luxembourg Palace, where the French Senate is housed. Commissioned by Marie de Médicis, widow of Henry IV, in the 17th century, the garden, nicknamed 'Luco' locally, blends French and English design with 106 statues and trees and shrubs filling 25 hectares of space. Expect massive chrysanthemum blossoms in October, as well as an orchid greenhouse, rose garden, free photography exhibitions and an apiary where you can learn about beekeeping.

🕐 *0800 to dusk daily* 🏠 *l'Odéon, 75006*
🔗 *www.senat.fr/visite/jardin* ✏ *Guided tour: 0930 (1st Weds of Apr-Oct, all Weds in June)*

"Look for the Fontaine Medicis, the state of the art of romanticism, by Marie de Médicis. And rent a boat to row at the central pond if you're bringing kids."
– Leslie Dubest, Un Plan Simple

8 **Hôtel National des Invalides**
Map B, P.102

Also referred to as Les Invalides, this prestigious complex exemplifies the scale and grandeur of French history. Created by Louis XIV in the 1670s to provide a shelter for disabled war veterans, the construct holds three museums; Musée de l'Ordre de la Libération, Musée des Plans-Reliefs and Musée de l'Armée – which houses the country's largest collection on the history of the French Military. Walk along the 500m lawn cascading from the building's exterior to view the luminescent golden globe topping the edifice.

🕐 Museums: 1000–1800 daily, ~1700 (Nov–Mar)
💲 €12/8.50 🏠 129 r. Grenelle, Invalides, 75007
URL www.musee-armee.fr
🖉 Special opening hours applied during Christmas and springtime holidays

"It's a place charged with history and I love history! Don't leave without seeing the impressive collection of uniforms and miniatures made by Charles Sandre."
– Patrick Norguet

9 Parc des Buttes-Chaumont
Map K, P.110

A quirky paradise on the outskirts of the city centre next to Belleville, Buttes-Chaumont, French for 'bald mount,' is Paris' steepest park. Built at Napoleon III's wish for more green zones, engineer Jean-Charles Alphand (1817–91) was responsible for the city's landscape design and directed the project, sprucing up the former 'bald mount' with rich vegetation, lakes, waterfalls and birdlife. The Temple de la Sibylle overlooking the park from above the lake is said to be a close replica of the Temple of Vesta in Tivoli, Italy.

🕐 *0700 till dusk daily*
📍 *1 r. Botzaris, Combat, 75019*

"A very sloppy park in a not so touristy area, and it's full of surprises. It's delightful to walk around or picnic on the grass when the weather is nice."
– Sophie Gateau

10 **Villa Savoye**
Map A, P.102

Known as one of the most important structures built in the 20th century, Villa Savoye fa-
mously embraces the mantra that "the house
is a machine for living." This Modernist country
house actualises originator Le Corbusier's
(1887-1965) idea of "Five Points of Architecture,"
swapping walls for pilotis (reinforced concrete
columns) alongside a roof garden, ribbon
windows, a liberal floor plan, and a façade
design free from structural restrictions. Take
RER A to Poissy Gare Sud, then bus route 50 ("la
Coudraie" direction) to "Villa Savoye."

🕐 *Tu-Su: 1000-1700, -1800 (May-Aug)*
💲 *€8/6.50* 🏠 *82, r. Villiers, Poissy, 78300*
📞 *+33 (0)1 3965 0106* 🔗 *www.villa-savoye.fr*
🔗 *Guided tour (EN): 1030, 1500 (W&F)*

*"It's a very good example of Le Corbusier's work.
Go there to spend a nice afternoon near Paris."*

– Julie Rothhahn

11 Siège du PCF, Espace Niemeyer
Map K, P.110

When approaching the French Communist Party Headquarters, visitors are greeted by a movie-like scene, with the building's curved curtain of glass bracketing a low rising white dome, often used as large conference hall. Completed in 1980 by Brazilian architect Oscar Niemeyer (1907–2012), with influences from his peers Jean Deroche, Paul Chemetov, Jean-Maur Lyonnet, and Jean Prouvé, this six-storey building has since doubled as a playground for fashion houses like Prada, Christian Dior, and Louis Vuitton. Take a prance across the rooftop café after snooping around the political party office.

🏠 *2 pl. Colonel Fabien, Combat, 75019*
🔗 *www.pcf.fr*

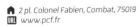

"Enter the building without being intimidated – most of the time, there are shows inside that are open to the public."
– Sophie Toporkoff

12 Citroën C42

Map C, P.103

You don't have to be a car fanatic to appreciate the phenomenal structure of this huge showroom. Cushioned between two traditional stone buildings on the Champs Élysées, which sees 80 million people walk along it each year, the Citroën display area is six storeys of modern glass and theatrical presence. An ambitious project, on entrance visitors will encounter eight vehicles stacked on each other, all of which can be viewed whilst ascending and descending the stairs that spiral around it. Views from the top give a unique vantage onto the famous avenue.

🕐 1000–2000 (Su–W), –2200 (Th–Sa)
🏠 42, av. Champs-Élysées, Faubourg-du-Roule, 75008
📞 +33 (0)1 5643 3670
URL www.c42paris.fr

"A very iconic architecture on the 'most beautiful avenue in the world', and the flagship showroom of a French car brand. I'm the architect!"

– Manuelle Gautrand

Cultural & Art Spaces

Art markets, cultural institutions and galleries

You'd be forgiven for thinking that the Paris art scene is all depictions of romantic scenes and oil painted nudes. However, there is an undoubted appetite for brave new thinking and creative innovation. Censorship and boundaries are exchanged for daring ideas and unpredictable line-ups. With a mix of permanent collections and temporary exhibitions, the diversity of the art on show is immeasurable.

The most excitement is to be found in the city's fringes, where fresh talent and underground initiatives combine to stage exciting shows and alternative performances. To get the best of the commercial offerings and thriving underground, pick and mix various exhibits and shows when planning your day; see a Monet at the Petit Palais (av. *Winston Churchill, Champs-Élysées, 75008*) before catching an evening art house film at Le Louxor (#15).

Thankfully in Paris, great food often comes with great art. When strolling through the myriad of creative spaces, don't forget to glance through the menus in the onsite cafés – Palais de Tokyo (#18) and La Halle Saint Pierre (#21) have fantastic lunch offerings.

Combo Culture Kidnapper, *Street artist*

I'm street artist. I paste posters in the street where people's faces are replaced by cartoon characters.

Grand Palais
033

COLONEL
Creative agency

We are a French design studio. We run a shop near Canal Saint-Martin with our own furniture and lighting collections.

Almasty
Creative agency

We are Charles Bataillie and Anna Apter, who have lived and worked at Almasty in Paris since 2010. We are art directors and illustrators who really like lemurs.

Centre
Pompidou
032

Le Louxor
034

Alex VI
Photographer

I am a French photographer deeply imbued with the architectural beauty of Paris. I do "light painting" at night, playing with fire, fireworks and electric lights while I shoot.

Point
Éphémère
038

Agathe Cordelle & Olivia Zeitline, *Creative duo*

Born and raised in Paris, we specialise in editorial strategies. We manage The Editorialist and publish reecrire.com that deals with topics around art and the society.

BETILLON / DORVAL-BORY
Architectural firm

This is where Raphaël Bétillon and Nicolas Dorval-Bory design public buildings and small experimental projects since 2009. Dorval-Bory also teaches at ENSA Normandie.

104
Centquatre
035

Palais de
Tokyo
039

Alexis Devevey
Artist, Rero Art

I create works between urban and conceptual art. Appropriation and self-censorship are key concepts in my exploration of image negation with struck out slogans.

Fondation Louis Vuitton 042

ARRO Studio
Creative agency

Founded in 2012 and based in Paris, ARRO is a product of Erik Arlen and Ludo Roth's mixed inspiration. ARRO sees design in a global way and works in multidisciplinary fields.

JUL & MAT
Director duo

JUL & MAT burst on the scene with "L'homme à 100 Têtes" and music videos. The team specialises in conceptual films and excels in graphic crafts and new narrative forms.

Backslash Gallery 040

Halle Saint Pierre 043

Sandrine Estrade Boulet
Artist & photographer

Hello, bonjour. Comment ça va? Une baguette s'il vous plait? When I was a girl, I used to lay on the slide for hours to watch clouds. Today, I have decided that I should never stop doing it.

La Maison Rouge 046

one more studio
Creative trio

Gaël Hugo, Charlotte Marcodini and Guilhem Moreau work separately in this studio space but share knowledge to conduct a radical vision in their field, from graphic to motion design.

Jules Julien
Artist & illustrator

I am Jules Julien. I've lived and worked in Paris in the Montmatre area for 13 years. Paris is a fantastic place for whoever loves art and fashion, enjoy!

Le Bal 044

12 MAIL 047

13 Centre Pompidou
Map E, P.106

With utilitarian features like pipes, plumbing and air vents running along its exterior, Centre Pompidou is a building well and truly turned 'inside out.' Inaugurated in 1977, over 150 million people have trailed through the six floors of this cultural labyrinth, the vision of architects Renzo Piano, Richard Rogers, and Gianfranco Franchini. Massive scale dominates, evident in the Musée National d'Art Moderne (4-5F), home to the over 65,000 pieces of art dating from 1905 onwards and the Bibliothèque publique d'information (1F) with its collection of 450,000 books. Get lost and cultured simultaneously.

🕐 1100-2200 (W-M), -2300 (Th)
💲 €14/11/free admission (monthly 1st Sundays)
🏠 pl. Georges-Pompidou, Saint-Gervais, 75004
📞 +33 (0)1 4478 1233 **URL** www.centrepompidou.fr

"When it's too crowded at the entrance, say you're going for Georges Restaurant and take the dedicated elevator from the Piazza. You'll save an hour wait."

– Combo Culture Kidnapper

14 Grand Palais

Le Grande Palais' majestic glass roof acts as a transparent sheath protecting the 40 events and 43 museum shops it houses. With a century's worth of exhibitions forming an impressive backlog, the iconic monument provokes wide-eyed wonderment upon arrival to its massive entry hall, the largest in Europe. Amongst the most impressive features is the Palais de la Découverte, the building's science museum and planetarium. Wander the centre to observe the capital's skies and learn about astronomy.

🕐 1000-2000 (W-M) 💲 Price varies with shows

🏠 3, av. Général Eisenhower, Champs-Élysées, 75008 (Entrance on av. Winston Churchill, av. Général Eisenhower & av. du Général Eisenhower)

📞 +33 (0)1 4413 1717

🔗 www.grandpalais.fr

"Go during the week to avoid weekend crowds."

– COLONEL

15 Le Louxor
Map F, P.106

Parisian and Egyptian aesthetics delightfully intertwined at this quaint cinema, nestled northwest of Gare du Nord. A former drug den, gay disco and 1980s club, the Art Deco movie theatre has been in existence since 1921 but was only recently restored to its former glory. Turquoise, gold and vibrant yellows enrich the interior of its three rooms, one of which, the "Youssef Chahine" houses 340 people across its orchestra section and balconies. Visit to view an unconventional range of international films.

🕐 Showtimes vary with shows
💲 €9.50/7.90/5.80/6/5
📍 170 blvd. Magenta, Saint Vincent de Paul, 75010
📞 +33 (0)1 4463 9696
🔗 www.cinemalouxor.fr

"It's a pre-war Egyptian-themed cinema. The architecture is very Art Deco, and they play art-house films."
– Almasty

104 Centquatre
Map K, P.110

A former house for Paris' municipal under-
takers, this 19th century building now offers
artistic facilities and a community culture
programme, leaving, thankfully, death a distant
memory. Following a 100-million-euro restora-
tion project, the centre has grown to become
one of the capital's most experimental and
fearless art initiatives. Across the 39,000sqm
space, expect to encounter alternative music
and concerts as well as theatre, dance, music,
cinema, digital and urban art by the city's most
innovative offspring.

🕐 1200-1900 (Tu-F), 1100- (Sa-Su)
💲 Price varies with programmes
🏠 5 r. Curial, La Villette, 75019
📞 +33 (0)1 5335 5000   URL www.104.fr
🎟 Buy tickets online or at venue 200/400
45mins before start time

"*They have really nice exhibitions and
art performance.*"

– Alex VI

17 Point Éphémère
Map K, P.110

Hosting a progressive culture and residency programme next to Canal Saint-Martin (#2), Point Éphémère is partly responsible for attracting a young fun crowd to the district. Foreign and homegrown talents hone and perfect their craft within this spacious arts facility, which stages a dance studio, a multimedia platform, music rehearsal rooms and a range of visual art studios. The 1920s warehouse also houses a rock bar/restaurant which dishes out comfort food and booze daily along the waterfront from noon. Exhibitions open from 2-7pm throughout the week with free admittance.

🕐 1200-0200 (M-Sa), -2200 (Su)
💲 Price varies with shows
🏠 200 quai de Valmy, Hôpital-Saint-Louis, 75010
📞 +33 (0)1 4034 0248 URL pointephemere.org

"Have a beer in one of Canal Saint-Martin's bars after a show."

– Agathe Cordelle & Olivia Zeitline

 **Palais de Tokyo**
Map C, P.102

Palais de Tokyo is a 7,800sqm concrete and steel shell with no permanent collection but the trendy spot has a penchant for unconventional art shows and cultural happenings. What goes on here is unpredictable and sporadic, a well-known place for a forward-thinking crowd in search of all things cutting edge. Temporary shows provide a party atmosphere that lasts until midnight. Also check out their great bookshop and walk on the esplanade for a different view of the much loved Eiffel Tower (#4).

🕐 1200–0000 (W–M), –1800 (Dec 24 & 31) 💲 €12/9
🏠 13 av. Président Wilson, Chaillot, 75116
📞 +33 (0)1 8197 3588
🔗 www.palaisdetokyo.com

"Unquestionably the best contemporary art centre in town."
– BETILLON / DORVAL-BORY

19 Backslash Gallery

Map D, P.105

It would be hard to overlook this matt black box nestled amongst the row of white town houses in the rising area of Arts et Métiers. The 250sqm space is a unique platform for new and daring work, boasting an energetic artist roster spanning varied generations and mediums, such as photography, sculpture, painting and video. Art lovers will revel in the gallery's continuously bold programme, which has already presented work on masculinity, exile and Afro American identity.

🕐 1400-1900 (Tu-Sa)
🏠 29 r. Notre-Dame de Nazareth, Arts et Métiers, 75003
📞 +33 (0)9 8139 6001
URL www.backslashgallery.com

"A must every month to discover the work of a new artist in a beautiful space. Contemporary gallery with a conceptual aspiration."

– Alexis Devevey, Rero Art

20 Fondation Louis Vuitton
Map J, P.109

The 2014 addition to the Paris museum family stands out instantly with its ambitious Frank Gehry architecture, leaving many to question what it seeks to express. Inside, the Fondation Louis Vuitton keeps up to that level of engagement throughout its diverse collection and exhibitions, created from the 1960s up to the current day. Contemplative, pop, expressionistic and musical, these art pieces seek constant critical reflection, break rules, and lead conversations on our ever changing world.

🕐 0900-2100 (M-Th, Sa-Su), -2300 (F)
💲 €16/10/5
🏠 8, av. du Mahatma Gandhi, Bois de Boulogne, 75116
📞 +33 (0)1 4069 9600 URL fondationlouisvuitton.fr
🔗 Hours extend from October to March. Shuttle service connects the Foundation & Place Charles de Gaulle: €2 (with admission tickets only)

"Paris has waited for a long time (since Ming Pei's Louvre Pyramid built in 1988) for a contemporary/bold building and site of this scale."
– ARRO Studio

21 Halle Saint Pierre
Map F, P.106

Venture to St. Peter's market for art on the fringes of the mainstream, an antidote to clean commercial offerings elsewhere. Specialising in *art brut* (raw art), La Halle Saint Pierre is a niche haven staging extensive folk art. The building plays host to a museum, modern art gallery, bookshop and café within its 19th century iron and glass walls and runs three temporary exhibitions per year. After a browse through the international work on show, grab a quiche and light salad at the cafe.

🕐 1100–1800 (M–F), –1900 (Sa), 1200–1800 (Su), Closed August weekends 💲 €9/7/6
🏠 2 r. Ronsard, Clignancourt, 75018
📞 +33 (0)1 4258 7289
🔗 www.hallesaintpierre.org

"For the choice of pop art and raw art on display."
– JUL & MAT

22 Le Bal
Map F, P.106

The value of the image in today's landscape is increasingly in question. Le Bal is passionate about creating a space where criticism and discussion on the representations of reality can flourish. An independent venue for all kinds of image – photography, video, film and new media, the two-floor exhibition space provides a series of talks, workshops and lectures throughout the year. For some quiet reflection, mill about the glass-walled terrace to overlook the busy neighbourhood.

🕐 1200–2100 (W), –2200 (Th), –2000 (F), 1100–2000 (Sa), –1900 (Su)
💲 €6/4
🏠 6 Impasse de la Défense, Grandes-Carrières, 75018
📞 +33 (0)1 4470 7550
🔗 www.le-bal.fr

"An excellent art space and café, and not too big. Highly recommended for its quality exhibitions, selection of books – sit and chill around."
– Sandrine Estrade Boulet

23 La Maison Rouge
Map H, P.108

Alternating between monographic and thematic exhibits, the 2000sqm space on boulevard de la Bastille is a provocative hot house. This blood red box often provides space for darker shows; "Tous Cannibales" was a daring exhibit on cannibalism, while "Memories of the Future" was an exhibition about death featuring artists like Albrecht Dürer (1471–1528) and Damien Hirst. The Rose Bakery round the corner offers a Parisian take on English grub, and is the go to spot for a bit of relief.

🕐 1100–1900 (W–Su), –2100 (Th)　💲 €10/7
🏠 10 blvd. la Bastille, Quinze-Vingts, 75012
📞 +33 (0)1 4001 0881
🔳 www.lamaisonrouge.org

"Taste the cakes at the entrance. They're very good!"
– Jules Julien

24 12 MAIL
Map D, P.104

An anarch take on the conventional white cube space, red bull's art initiative isn't about big names or big prices but instead embraces controversial ideas and uncensored experimentation. Open since 2009 and located in the second arrondissement, 12 MAIL has given curatorial reign to Elisabeth Arkhipoff's fictional band "Sport Hit Paradise" as well the editors of independent tattoo magazine *Sang Bleu*. Keep an eye on their blog to keep up to date on their next gritty instalment.

🕐 1400-1800 (W-F)
🏠 12 r. Mail, Mail, 75002
✉ infos@12mail.fr
URL www.12mail.fr

"It's rapidly reaching the edges/margin of contemporary creation."
– one more studio

Markets & Shops

Local designs, French foodstuffs and select art books

Parisians seem to have perfected all facets of consumption. The habit of eating, dressing and buying well manifests in a capital laced with beautiful boutiques and exceptional produce. Vintage obsessives will find Paris naturally demonstrates flair for both well-archived fashion artefacts that retail either cheaply or require exceptional investment. Concept stores have also made their mark though smaller shops such as L'Atelier Beau Travail (#25) and FrenchTrotters (#32) also provide exclusive brands and plenty of character. Spare a day for Le Marais, a charming district where medieval architecture, art, fashion and modern cuisine interweave. Besides the shops highlighted in this section, a visit to Yvon Lambert Bookshop and Gallery (*108 r. Vieille du Temple, Le Marais, 75003*) and Florence Loewy by artists (*9 r. de Thorigny, Le Marais, 75003*) unveils exciting ranges of artist books, Popelini (*29 r. Debelleyme, Enfants Rouges, 75003*) boasts unforgettable choux à la crème, and Beaucoup (*3 r. Froissard, Le Marais, 75003*) offers playful dining chic. Boulevards Saint Michel and Saint Germain are famous for historic old cafés and bistros and are perfect for grabbing authentic Parisian treats. But don't be a slave to The Guide – in Paris some of the best discoveries are made simply by getting lost in its streets.

Hélène Georget
Graphic designer

I'm a French print designer and I work for fashion brands and newspapers as a freelancer. I've been living in Paris for six years and I love it!

Ofr.
054

Alexandra Bruel
Artist

I studied graphic design at the Gobelins School and work mainly with plasticine. I'm represented by Handsome Frank and work for clients across the advertising and design sectors.

Christelle Ménage
Graphic designer

I am graphic designer with a big love for systems because they can be applied to any medium and concept, in print or web, with wood or clay. What a nice playground in life! :)

L'Atelier
Beau Travail
052

Un Regard
Moderne
055

Coco aka Forget Me Not
Graphic artist & designer

Fine art graduate who has been a communication consultant for multiple top fashion designers. Coco travelled extensively in Asia and the US before co-creating Inoui in 2004.

Comptoir de
l'Image
058

Jean-Yves Lemoigne
Photographer

I'm an advertising photographer and my surrealistic photos turn routines into another dimension. I work with top agencies like W+K and BBH. and magazines like *WAD* and *BKRW*.

Carine Brancowitz
Illustrator

Carine Brancowitz spent her childhood in France, devoting her time to music and painting. With simple tools, she draws to combine the purity and passion of adolescent anxiety.

THANX GOD
I'M A V.I.P.
056

Hôtel Drouot
059

Diane Pernet
Fashion journalist

Diane is considered a visionary and a pioneer among fashion industry circles. She is the founder of fashion film festival ASVOFF and runs now famous blog www.ASVOF.com.

French-Trotters
061

Tove Johansson
Designer

I'm a Swedish girl living in Paris for eight years working in fashion, interior and printmaking for textiles and stationery. I'm currently developing my own line with focus on print and colour.

Studio L'Étiquette
Creative agency

Founded in 2012 by Alma de Ricou and Manon Engel, Studio L'Étiquette believes in the power of images. We work on disciplines from fashion to animation and set design.

Ragtime
060

Guerrisol
062

Elise Darblay
Film director

As an ex-anthropologist, I am profoundly interested in new culture. Now I direct documentary films and music videos with my lover, and raise two kids in Paris – until we move.

Marché Bastille
064

Antoine+Manuel
Graphic design duo

Antoine and Manuel met in a prep art school in 1984 and started working under "Antoine+Manuel" in 1993. 2009 saw their retrospective exhibition in Paris and Hong Kong.

Chic & Artistic
Creative agency

Chic & Artistic is Corinne Black and Axel d'Harcourt who collaborate with the entertainment and high-end cultural world. Their specialties span graphic design and motion design.

Le Marché d'Aligre
063

Marché des Enfants Rouges
065

25 L'Atelier Beau Travail
Map O, P.111

Delphine Dunoyer, Céline Saby, Rachel Péloquin and Bonana van Mil are the four young creatives that fashioned this vibrant little paradise on rue de la Mare. Each Saturday, the public can peer into the world of this mini workshop, an ever-expanding collection of colourful trinkets, homeware, art and clothing. Unique and handmade, the group also promotes the work of young emerging artists in design and fashion in curated thematic exhibitions. Be sure to purchase one of their printed silk scarves as a souvenir.

🕐 1400–1900 (Sa)
🏠 67 r. la Mare, Belleville, 75020
📧 contact@beautravail.fr
URL www.beautravail.fr

"I love to stroll around the streets of this area. There are lots of little shops, an underground library and free markets."

– Hélène Georget

26 Ofr.
Map G, P.107

Artists, designers, filmmakers, publishers and fine art students all flock to this beautiful little art bookshop eager to discover rare and limited edition finds which span new photography books, cult fashion magazines and lifestyle goods. For 20 years, the Thumerelle siblings Alexandre and Marie have successfully composed a stimulating setting, shaping the store into a quintessential French community space where patrons and friends convene for inspiration and style. View art in the back room where exhibitions rotate at least twice a month.

🕐 1000-2000 (M–Sa), 1400-1900 (Su)
🏠 20, r. Dupetit-Thouars, Le Marais, 75003   ☎ +33 (0)1 4245 7288
URL www.ofrsystem.com

"Take your time. This is a great gallery and bookstore that breathes creation."

– Alexandra Bruel

27 Un Regard Moderne

Map E, P.106

Stacks and stacks of books make up the fabric of this quaint little shop. Walls are barely visible behind the tall blocks of counter culture archives, housing an extensive collection of independent prints spanning themes such as surrealism, fetishism, erotica and outsider art. Only three to four people can fit into the store, the brainchild of avant-garde owner Jacques Noel, at any one time. Nuzzled on rue Gît-le-Coeur (The Street Where your Heart Lay Down) enter with an open mind and see what you find.

🕐 1130–2000 (M–Sa)
🏠 10 r. Gît-le-coeur, Monnaie, 75006
📞 +33 (0)1 4329 1393
URL www.unregardmoderne.com

"You might not be searching for anything in particular but you will find it anyway. A nice little chat with the very interesting and literate owner is an added bonus."

– Christelle Ménage

28 THANX GOD I'M A V.I.P.

Map D, P.105

You will notice the display. Vibrantly designed, wondrously detailed, ever changing and oh-so fun, THANX GOD I'M A V.I.P. reveals its quirky character before you even enter. Its gem of a vintage collection comes in a rainbow array of colours that can be classic, casual and funky, all with their own individual energy and always in style. Described as "when vintage meets music", the store also built a strong community around itself by being part of the Parisian nightlife, hosting night outs with music and fashion lovers. Go on then, pick out an outfit and have a dance.

🕑 1400-2000 (M-Sa)
🏠 12 r. de Lancry, 75010
📞 +33 (0)1 4203 0209
URL thanxgod.com
✒ Shop may take summer breaks.

"This place carries amazing vintage selections. The basement has great bargains!"

– Coco aka Forget Me Not

29 Comptoir de l'Image
Map H, P.108

Stuffed with rare photography publications and old fashion magazines, from books on Helmut Newton and Henri Cartier Bresson to '90s *The Face* magazines and '80s Italian *Vogues*, Comptoir de l'Image has become a favoured research point for designers such as John Galliano and Marc Jacobs. The place is tiny but these physical paper treasures hold a vitality that online image hunting cannot touch.

🕐 1200–1900 (M-Sa)
🏠 44 r. Sévigné, Le Marais, 75003
📞 +33 (0)1 4272 0392

"*This is a great spot for book lovers. It is a small shop but you can find some very rare gems. The owner is really nice and has a great knowledge about fashion.*"
– Jean-Yves Lemoigne

30 Hôtel Drouot (Auction House)
Map D, P.104

Hôtel Drouot, the largest auction house in Europe, houses 100 auctioneers and hosts 3,000 auctions every year across four locations and 21 exposition halls. Since 1852, a vast range of fine art and antiques have set off out of its grasp and into the hands of novices and experts alike. If auctions are new to you, don't be deterred. Browse through the museum-like hall and observe how experienced art and antique dealers work their magic if you're not keen to enter the bidders circle yourself.

🕐 1100-1800 (M-Sa), - 2100 (Th)
📍 9 r. Drouot, Faubourg-Montmarte, 75009
📞 +33 (0)1 4800 2020
URL www.drouot.com

"The best place to chase antiquities, furniture, and paintings in Paris. Go up the stairs and start wandering from room to room."
– Carine Brancowitz

31 Ragtime
Map E, P.106

Ragtime, in fact, provides everything but rags. The vintage store offers a stunning collection of haute couture from the 20th century. Rare Dior dresses, Balmain suits and Chanel bags are in absolute perfect condition. The collection is curated by clothing expert Françoise Auget and prices are steep with dresses retailing for around €1,000. Despite the heavy price tags, it might be well worth investing in a perfect piece of artisanal genius, even with no occasion to wear it!

🕐 1430–1900 (M-Sa)
🏠 23 r. Echaudé, Saint-Germain-des-Prés, 75006
📞 +33 (0)1 5624 0036

"It is possible to have the pieces altered to your measurements. Be sure to check the hours, opens in afternoons and closed on Mondays."
– Diane Pernet

32 FrenchTrotters
Map H, P.109

Two former photography students Carole and Clarent Dehlouz squeeze their knowledge of New York, Tokyo and London into this concept store. The result is a cosmopolitan oasis presenting exclusive brands such as Acne, Opening Ceremony, Our Legacy, and American Vintage. Alongside the international brands, FrenchTrotters have released their own clothing range for men and women. The store is a fusion of Parisian style and global influences. Their chic aesthetic also extends to furniture, fragrance and art, also available online.

🕙 1130–1930 (Tu–Sa)
🏠 30 r. Charonne, Roquette, 75011
☎ +33 (0)1 4700 8435
🔗 www.frenchtrotters.fr

"Nice shop with a good shop concept; nice selection of designers and products, where fashion and lifestyle meets."
– Tove Johansson

33 # Guerrisol
Map F, P.106

Trendy hipsters and elderly ladies rummage side by side through this wonderfully cheap secondhand shop. Arguably the best vintage spot in Paris, Guerrisol offers gems in abundance – if you put in a little elbow grease. Leather boots, furs, trench coats and old levis, priced from three to €20, are scattered everywhere, and are perhaps a wise alternative to the more expensive stores in Le Marais. With its contents constantly on rotation, it may pay off to visit as often as possible to get the most out of the regular influx of distinctive clothing.

🕐 1000–1930 daily
🏠 17 blvd. Rochechouart, Rochechouart, 75009
☎ +33 (0)1 4526 1312
URL guerrisol.fr

"A real secondhand clothes shop! No zoning system means it's quite a challenge to find what you want but it's really worth digging into it."
– Studio L'Étiquette

34 Le Marché d'Aligre
Map H, P.109

One of the oldest covered markets in Paris, this mid-19th century structure is home to bustling stalls offering everything from fresh fruit and vegetables to foie gras and caviar. With a wonderful riot of vocal stall owners and excited customers, Le Marché d'Aligre is full of life and steeped in history. Many of the stall owners are third or fourth generation, following the footsteps of their parents and grandparents. Venture to the site on mornings during weekdays to explore the labyrinth with sufficient elbowroom.

🕘 0900–1300, 1600–1930 (Tu–F), 0900–1300, 1530–1930 (Sa), 0900–1330 (Sun)
🏠 pl. d'Aligre, Jardin des Plantes, 75012

"*Go to Brunon the butcher and take whatever is on offer, have a mint tea at a little café nearby Le Pen-Ty or oysters at the Baron Rouge in the R-months.*"

– Elise Darblay

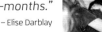

35 Marché Bastille
Map H, P.108

Twice a week, a large dose of sensory indulgence lands at boulevard Richard Lenoir. Offering a myriad of seasonal produce, Bastille Food Market is a treasure trove for food enthusiasts. Towers of fruit and vegetables sit next to local cheeses, fresh fish and various hot bites from French, Lebanese, Italian and Indian cooks. Colossal in scale, often with price tags to match, the market is a go to place for small luxuries. Visit on Saturday to browse through a selection of arts, crafts, unique jewellery and clothing.

🕐 0700–1430 (Th), –1500 (Su)
🏠 blvd. Richard Lenoir, Roquette, 75011
📞 +33 (0)1 4324 7439
🔗 equipement.paris.fr/marche-bastille-5477

"A fantastic experience to discover French food and Parisians. Wake up early to avoid the crowd, best around 9–10am."

– Antoine+Manuel

36 Marché des Enfants Rouges

Map G, P.107

Across the 2000sqm of this historical market are hundreds of traders selling an impressive source of fresh produce and global cuisine. Established in 1628 and taking its name after the orphanage that formerly occupied the space, Le Marché des Enfants Rouges reopened in 2000 after locals fought for its return. From Tuesday to Sunday, hundreds of Parisians flock to traders offering exceptional wine, cheese, breads, and meats. For those in search of indulgence, look for the famous oyster vendors and get a taste of oceanic delight.

🕑 *Opening hours vary with shops, closed Mondays*
🏠 *39 r. Bretagne, Le Marais, 75003*

"There is a big number of stalls where you can actually eat. The Japanese is specially good."

– Chic & Artistic

Restaurants & Cafés

Authentic French, modern fusion and fancy desserts

Baguettes, croissants, frog legs and snails are the classics of French cuisine, but to minimise the region's variety and complexity is to really miss out. International influences often merge with traditional dishes and are finished with quintessential Parisian flair but fail to overshadow the more traditional gastronomic outlets that characterise many street corners. For an authentic dine-in experience, start your journey with French delicacies, from the simple yet unforgettable sandwiches (casse-croûte) and cheese at Le Bistrot des Halles (#41) or stews at Chez Denise (#40), to contemporary desserts and pastries created by Christophe Michalak (#45). For a taste of modern French culinary, fight for a seat at Septime (#48), and pop into Breizh Café (*100, r. Vielle du Temple, Le Marais, 75003*) for paper-thin crêpes filled with Valhona chocolate. Travellers should bear in mind that most French kitchens are pretty serious about their afternoon break, so play it safe and arrive for lunch before 1.30pm to avoid getting shut out. In any case, a picnic in the city's public parks or along the water is a leisurely activity on warm days and almost as impressive. Put together a basket with local fruits and baked goods from the top picks listed in *Count to 10*.

Marion Laurens
Art director, Artworklove studio

I'm French and co-founder of communication and design agency, Artworklove. My passion lies within crafting original ideas through art direction, typography and digital media.

Gioia Mia
071

Elise Morin
Artist

I am an artist and designer who lives and works in Paris. I do site-specific installation art that utilises everyday manufactured materials.

Jules Faure
Art director & photographer

I studied graphic design at Olivier de Serres and am now an art director for fashion magazines. Born and raised in Paris, I love a romantic way of living, film noir, dirty music and good food.

Hôtel Edgar
070

Café de
l'Industrie
072

Jolie Cherie
Band

Jolie Cherie is an electro-pop trio featuring Etienne de Champfleury, Samir Alliche and Melina Duval. Our music is like "menthe à l'eau" – sweet, refreshing and not dizzy.

Le Bistrot
des Halles
074

Amélie Falière
Illustrator

I am native to Bourgogne, and I came in Paris nine years ago to pursue my art studies. I draw for young readers. I live in the 15th arrondissement with my love and two cats.

Sarah Andelman
Creative director, colette

Along with my mother Colette Rousseaux, I opened colette in 1997, now a prestigious meeting point for offbeat fashion, music, food and design worldwide.

Chez Denise
073

Kunitoraya
075

Ruben Brulat
Photographer

Since owning my first camera in 2008, I've been capturing the beauty blending man and the nature in the Primates or the bare buildings of Paris. I've just published a book, *Sharing Paths*.

Chez Nénesse
078

Pleix
Creative agency

Pleix is a community of graphic designers, 3D artists, and musicians who mix digital skills to gain greater freedom for various projects. We are seven individuals, all based in Paris.

David Charhon
Filmmaker

I'm French. My early work as a director and screenwriter includes short films and commercials and my latest feature is *De l'autre côté du périph* (2012) starring Omar Sy.

Le Petit Marché
076

Café Michalak
079

Jure Kotnik
Founder, Arhitektura Jure Kotnik

With offices in Ljubljana and Paris, I work from research to architectural design. I also publish specialised books and teach at Ecole Speciale d'Architecture, Paris.

Derrière
081

The Imaginers
Creative agency

We are an imaginative team who "imagineers" for ad campaigns and boutique design, in Europe, USA and Asia. We also own a fashion trade show MAN and WOMAN in Paris and NYC.

Kanako B. Koga
Fashion director

Japanese born, Paris-based stylist and fashion director for *Code Magazine* (NL). I also take on advertising and fashion shows and I'm a mother of two.

Le Bouchon des Batignolles
080

Septime
082

 Hôtel Edgar
Map D, P.105

Found in the quirky neighbourhood Sentier, an old prominent textile manufacturing district and new centre for Parisian Internet start-ups, this boutique hotel houses a stunning restaurant with a sun-kissed terrace and great food. The eatery provides an unexpected Anglophone menu, with international influences, and a sea-infused theme. Expect polished fish and chips, breaded calamari and smoked herring among others. Begin the morning with a plate of organic eggs Benedict on the terrace or converse with friends over Roumégous oysters and Bordier butter at lunch.

🕑 1130–1500 daily, 1930–2300 (M–Sa)
🏠 31 r. d'Alexandrie, Bonne Nouvelle, 75002
📞 +33 (0)1 4041 0569 🔳 edgarparis.com

EDGAR
HÔTEL & RESTAURANT

"A great hotel with an amazing restaurant right in the middle of Paris. Check out room 12, it's mine!"
– Marion Laurens, Artworklove studio

38 Gioia Mia
Map D, P.104

A little piece of Italy in the heart of Paris, Gioia Mia represents the fine cuisine of the Puglia region of southern Italy. Everything here is as authentic as it gets but without being pedantic, as founding French-Italian chef Arnaud Gioia is keen to uphold the area's definition of good food and good service with the greatest joy and humour. Enjoy the beautiful energy of the people and the charming place along with simple but refined menu. Their burrata is wonderfully delicate and creamy. Miss it and you'll regret it.

🕐 1200–1430, 1930–2130 (M–F)
🏠 61 r. de Provence, 75009
📞 +33 (0)1 4526 6130

"Don't miss their burrata or follow Arnaud's advice. I go there every week, so maybe we'll enjoy a glass of Prosecco together."

– Elise Morin

39 Café de l'Industrie
Map H, P.108

A magnet for local artists and creatives, this little hangout always gets crowded fast. Adorned with old masks, exotic paintings and French colonial treasures, the one room venue has a delightfully quirky and relaxed vibe akin to a neighbourhood canteen that is always warm and inviting. The limited menu celebrates traditional and typically French dishes at competitive prices. Try roast meats, steak tartar, duck confit and perhaps a devilish chocolate fondant for the sweet-toothed. Open till the early hours, the café welcomes visitors in need of an early morning coffee as well as a late night cocktail.

🕐 0900–2345 daily
🏠 16 r. Saint-Sabin, Roquette, 75011
📞 +33 (0)1 4700 1353

"The dishes of the day are always tasty so come several times!"
– Jules Faure

40 Chez Denise
Map E, P.106

With doors open till 5am, this bustling restaurant welcomes visitors at virtually anytime during weekdays, and can be found in the heart of the old butchers district. The classic bistro, wonderfully informal and laidback, serves copious amounts of food and still has its menu written in "Louchebem" (French butchers' slang from the 1950s). Chez Denise has a different special each day but they are mainly known for rich and juicy meat dishes – their veal kidneys with mustard sauce, beef flank steak, boiled beef stew and Charolaise rib roast beef are legendary. All dishes are best enjoyed with their house Brouilly wine.

🕐 1200–1500, 1930–0500 (M–F)
🏠 5 r. Prouvaires, Les Halles, 75001
📞 +33 (0)1 4236 2182

"When you order your piece of 'Baba au rhum', don't be surprised to see the waiter bringing you a whole bottle of rum with the cake. They serve generously!"
– Jolie Cherie

🕐 0700–2100 (M–Sa), –2200 (Tu)
🏠 15 r. Halles, Les Halles, 75001
🕐 +33 (0)1 4236 9169

41 Le Bistrot des Halles
Map E, P.106

With its authentic Parisian café look, Bistrot des Halles could easily escape your notice, but this charismatic bistro has survived the great transformations of Les Halles for good reason. Taken over by Jean-Pierre and Isabelle Breud in 1999, the café revives the glory of the old-time marketplace with unpretentious traditional dishes –"*casse-croûtes* (French sandwiches, read *kas.krut*)," homemade bites and excellent cheese and charcuterie boards, as well as duck confit and tartare steaks from the kitchen. Whether you choose to be seated at the terrace or relax inside, don't go without trying their wines.

"*Never ask for a sandwich there. They prefer to call it casse croûte because it's real French food. Don't go if you're in a hurry. Service can be slow.*"
– Amélie Falière

42 Kunitoraya
Map D, P.104

Since making a splash on rue Sainte-Anne, which is packed with Japanese eateries, Kunitoraya's second venue similarly produces mouth-watering gourmet udon, with owner and chef Masafumi Nomoto personally preparing the dough. Besides the specialised udon menu, Kunitoraya also serves original *onigiri* (rice balls), rice dishes and *bento* at lunch, and lavish fusion entrées, grills and fries at dinner. The corner shop is a more upbeat noodle house with communal tables and open kitchen, while the other has a more upmarket space with a classic Frenchie vibe.

🕐 1215–1430, 1930–2230 (Tu–Sa)
🏠 1 & 5 r. Villedo, Palais-Royal, 75001
📞 +33 (0)1 4703 0774
🔗 www.kunitoraya.com

"It was a beautiful old French brasserie before it's transformed into a Japanese restaurant. Go for the onigiri."

– Sarah Andelman, colette

43 Le Petit Marché

Map H, P.108

A short walk away from Place des Vosges (#1), Le Petit Marché offers a fusion menu with Asian influences. Candles, mirrored walls and wooden tables make for an old school vibe, however the clean and modern offering of flash-fried tuna and *Chinoise* salad exemplifies a forward-thinking tonality. Go for the vegetarian risotto with basil, coriander, cream and green beans for a light main or try the thick pork fillet with Sichuan spices and caramelised apples for a heartier meal. Whilst the lunch menu is more than affordable, be prepared to spend a little more for an evening dinner.

🕐 1200–1500 (M–F), –1600 (Sa–Su); 1900–0200 (M–Su)
🏠 9 r. Béarn, Le Marais, 75003
📞 +33 (0)1 4272 0667
URL *www.lepetitmarche.eu*

"A *cosy delight of Paris, mixing food and tastes from here and elsewhere. It just transports you.*"

– Ruben Brulat

44 Chez Nénesse
Map G, P.107

Chez Nénesse is an understated destination that sits quietly on a backstreet in Le Marais, with quaint lace curtains concealing retro décor. Head cook Chef Roger Leplu consistently demonstrates his Michelin star expertise through a menu of homely re-creations. The wooden stove in the centre of the restaurant simmers generous portions of stewed snails with mushrooms and rich onion soup. Unashamedly old fashioned, the restaurant's original owner has been replaced by a family from Le Sart however genuine Parisian gastronomy still remains its priority.

🕐 1200-1430, 2000-2215 (M-F)
🏠 17 r. Saintonge, Le Marais, 75003
📞 +33 (0)1 4278 4649

 "My favourites are 'boeuf à la ficelle' (beef on a string), their famous French fries and as dessert – 'mille feuilles (Napoleon)'!"
– Pleix

45 Café Michalak
Map D, P.105

Renowned pastry chef and modern-day Willy Wonka, Christophe Michalak has created a pastry school and takeaway spot where childhood fantasies come to life. With a repertoire of over 3000 recipes, the cake shop formulates their stunning confections fresh every morning to sell on the day. Inventions such as the chocolate-shaped K7 videotape stuffed with chocolate cereal, hazelnut and peanut praline are mouth-wateringly intense. Grab a Kosmik (a potted creamy dessert – pick the chocolate hazelnut *fleur-de-sel* flavour) and indulge in the nearby Square Montholon.

🕐 1000–1900 (M-Sa)
📍 60 r. Faubourg Poissonnière, Porte Saint-Denis, 75010
📞 +33 (0)1 4246 1045
🔗 christophemichalak.com

"We share the same passions for a taste for excellence! You'll get it when you see the classic circular 'Paris Brest' become a wavering 'Paris Montaigne.'"

– David Charhon

46 **Le Bouchon des Batignolles**
Map F, P.106

Located in the heart of Batignolles, a few strides away from Place de Clichy, Le BB serves Mediterranean tapas and wines in an elegant intimate setting. A sweet buffet consisting of fresh bread, Corsican honey, jams and nutella will satisfy sweet cravings that strike in the morning, whilst a traditional selection of mini pastries, cheeses, quiche *du jour* with fresh seasonal fruit juice works fittingly for a casual Sunday brunch. For something a bit more formal, order fresh cod, aioli and mashed potatoes and follow with their smooth panna cotta.

🕐 1900–0200 daily
🏠 2 r. Lemercier–14 r. Dames, Batignolles, 75017
📞 +33 (0)1 4293 5869
🔗 paris17.lebb.fr

"If you have trouble with choosing just one main dish, this is absolutely the place for you."

– Jure Kotnik, Arhitektura Jure Kotnik

47 Derrière

Map D, P.105

This apartment style venue certainly is an unconventional restaurant setting; diners are free to eat their meal in the lounge, dining room, screening room or bedroom. Countering the eccentric atmosphere, Chef Lionel Delage offers a minimal take on French cuisine, serving plenty of light salads and hearty dishes such as beef cheek bourguignon and creamy foie gras terrine. Sitting on the edge of the Marais district between restaurant 404 and Andy Wahloo (#55), all run by Mourad Mazouz, owner of Sketch and Momo in London, the unmarked door opens up a dining experience that's much like eating at a friend house.

🕐 *1200-1430, 2000-2330 (M-F), 2000-2330 (Sa), 1200-1630, 2000-2300 (Su)*
🏠 *69 r. Gravilliers, Arts et Métiers, 75003*
📞 *+33 (0)1 44 61 91 95*
🔗 *derriere-resto.com*

"There is a hidden room on 1F, which you need to go through a mirror to access."

– The Imaginers

48 Septime
Map H, P.109

At 27, chef/proprietor Bertrand Grébaut is the youngest French chef to win a Michelin star, and brings pure, clean cuisine to Septime. Together with partner Théo Pourriat, the restaurant creates dishes that combine seasonal cooking with high quality ingredients, inspired both by Grébaut's Asian travels and his extensive experience under legendary cook Alain Passard. Visually refined dishes such as *veal au lait* with salty trout eggs or *fromage blanc* ice cream on pumpkin puree are a testament to Septime's straightforward preparations, which aim at fresh and honest flavours.

🕐 1215–1400 (T–F), 1930–2200 (M–F)
🏠 80 r. Charonne, Roquette, 75011
📞 +33 (0)1 43 67 38 29
URL septime-charonne.fr

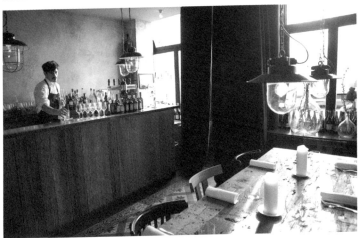

"I love their Ricotta with anchovy and grilled buckwheat seeds, as much as its casual atmosphere. And, the price is cheap!"
– Kanako B. Koga

Nightlife

Costume nights, voguish clubs, theatres and jazz

Dispel any preconceived ideas of an uptight scene dominated by bourgeois fashion folk – the truth stands that Paris nightlife is all accommodating. From makeshift party bunkers to luxe members-only clubs, all tastes and incomes are expansively catered for. Each district has its own unique flavour, so avoid getting too attached to a particular area or you may miss out. Le Marais offers a liberating atmosphere with the city's most popular gay and lesbian bars strewn across its streets; Bastille is a hotspot for lively Latin clubs whilst Oberkampf-menilmontant, with its cluster of trendy bars is hipster central. Ease gently into the evening watching the sunset from the huge wooden terrace at Wanderlust inside Les Dock (#3) while minimal techno and house music booms in the background. Le Crazy Horse Paris (*12 av. George V, Champs-Élysées, 75008*) provides an authentic cabaret experience with tantalising shows that have featured the likes of Dita Von Teese and Pamela Anderson. Or set off to Le Bellevilloise (*19–21 r. Boyer, Belleville, 75020*) for an arts and culture infused night – the club-cum-concert venue regularly hosts music festivals and exhibitions and the restaurant is perfect for a lazy supper. Partygoers should bear in mind that queues start around 8pm, making an early arrival a must in most instances. It's also advisable to double check door policy and rules regarding dress code to save unnecessary embarrassment!

Renaud Duc
Fashion designer

Founder of the brand Midnight Rendez-vous, DJ, party planner. Having lived in Paris for over 11 years, I'm fed up with the subway and complain... like a genuine Parisian.

Parc de la Villette
090

Fabienne Rivory
Designer & photographer

I am currently exploring interactions between photography and painting, real world and imagination, memories and reality through project 'Labokoff.'

Stéphane Massa-Bidal
Art director

I'm a hair icon, art director, cook, Frenchie, dad, genius brain owner, curator, co-owner of Les Contrepétographes. My work performs an interaction between images and text.

House of Moda Party
088

MAMA Shelter
091

David Porchy
Artist

He loves images and he collects and works with them. His drawings and photographs capture the strangeness of our world and of what ought to be called 'the real and its doubles'.

Rosa Bonheur
093

Violaine & Jérémy
Art directors & illustrators

We are in love with each other and Paris. We have a typical French way of living: everything is about good food, good wine and good cheese (sorry for the cliché). We travel a lot.

Isabelle Chapuis
Photographer

I am a photographer living in Paris. My work combines art and fashion. I love inner creative movements and going abroad, visiting other countries.

Le Trianon
092

New Morning
094

Flaminia Saccucci
Fashion designer

I am from Rome and a Central Saint Martins graduate who started off at Givenchy, Paris. Now I always travel between Italy and Paris for my freelance work.

Carmen
096

Violaine d'Harcourt
Product & furniture designer

A designer who combines work experiences abroad to give real life to her drawings and work. D'Harcourt studied in Paris and Milan with a Master's degree in industrial design.

Karine + Oliver
Photographer duo

We are Karine Welter and Oliver Rust – two crazy, passionate photographers living between Paris and Zurich.

Andy
Wahloo
095

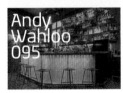

Bus
Palladium
097

Wanja Ledowski
Graphic designer & typographer

German-born graphic designer and typography teacher who lives and works in Paris. After cooperations with different design offices I started Wanja Ledowski-Studio in 2009.

Le Non_Jazz
100

Mehdi Hercberg
Artist

My work focuses on monsters and creatures that are strange, pop but sometimes cute. Also known as Shoboshobo, I have a strong bond with Japan, where I visit as often as I can.

Alexandre Plicque-Gurlitt, *Art director*

I am an art director, currently working on a variety of print and new-media-based projects including the production of AD campaigns, videos, website, logotypes, and brand identities.

Le Comptoir
Général
098

Silencio
101

087

49 House of Moda Party
Map G, P.107

Misfits, freaks and outsiders flee to this boisterous party night, one of the most talked about events in Paris. Centring on themes such as "Pharaohs" and "Lost in Space," underground artists and DJs from all over the world take the stage for nights of performances dedicated to liberating your inner diva. Glitter, elaborate costumes and heavy bass create a ferocious atmosphere of careless energy and shameless fun. Visit the House of Moda blog for regular updates on their next theme and any future headliners.

🕐 💲 *Showtime & price vary with event*
🏠 *Regular venue: La Java, 105 r. Faubourg du Temple, La Folie–Méricourt, 75010*
📞 *houseofmodaparis@gmail.com*
🔗 *houseofmoda.tumblr.com*

"Clearly the best party in Paris, not only because I am the one organising it but all night creatures will gather there to party! ...Dress up!"

– Renaud Duc

 50 Parc de la Villette
Map K, P.110

Spanning a 55-hectare plot, Parc de la Villette inhabits a site formally designated for old abattoirs, architect Bernard Tschumi won an international competition to design the park in 1982, and subsequently helped design a multifaceted wonderland filled with playgrounds, cultural spaces and theatres. Stroll along the Canal de l'Ourcq before visiting major venues Cite des Sciences et de l'Industrie and La Geode. During the summer months, attend the open-air film festival, held from mid-July to mid-August.

🕐 Ⓢ *24hrs, showtime & price vary with programmes*
🏠 *211 av. Jean Jaurès, Pont-de-Flandres, 75019*
📞 *+33 (0)1 4003 7575*
URL *www.villette.com*

 "It's the largest urban cultural park in the capital. Visit the nearby science museum with your children in the daytime."

– Fabienne Rivory, Labokoff

 MAMA Shelter

Map Q, P.111

More than just rooms and restaurants, Mama Shelter is a true urban refuge of life and encounters. Previously the village of Charonne, Philippe Starck turned the offbeat corner into a hip drinking hole for Parisians and tourists alike. Under the low chalkboard ceilings, the laid-back lounge and cocktail bar are crammed with people enjoying authentic French regional cuisine alongside the extensive wine list and live music. Chill with breeze at the rooftop; Sunday brunch there is especially popular. A fan of game? Drown yourself with their table football and table tennis!

🕐 Daily (Restaurant) 0800–1030, 1200–1430, 2000–2330 (Bar) 1230–0130, Rooftop closed in winter
🏠 109 rue de Bagnolet 75020
📞 +33 (0)1 4348 4848
URL www.mamashelter.com

"Design, beautiful hotel too, Sunday buffet brunch was cool. Designed by Philippe Starck, decoration is very funny. The place is like a lounge. The music is also amazing with a live DJ."

– Stéphane Massa-Bidal

52 Le Trianon
Map F, P.106

Initially starting out as a "café-concert" in 1894, a theatre and music hall in 1902 and then a cinema in 1939, Le Trianon re-emerged in 2010 as a full amalgamation of its extensive history. With a 1,500 capacity theatre, the celebrated music venue has played host to classical concerts and international musicians such as M.I.A., Goldfrapp, and Deep Purple. A long-time artist hangout dating back to the early 20th century, an adjacent café-bar, Le Petit Trianon, serves prime quality Parisian ham and artisanal mustard among other delicious brasserie fare daily from 10am till midnight.

 🕐 30 mins before scheduled shows 🏠 80 blvd. Rochechouart, Clignancourt, 75018 📞 +33 (0)1 4492 7800 URL www.letrianon.fr

 "This old theatre and ballroom is surely the most beautiful concert place in Paris. Eat/drink at Le Petit Trianon next door."

– David Porchy

53 Rosa Bonheur

Map K, P.110

Wooden benches, plastic lawn chairs and a quaint café sit huddled together in the heart of Buttes Chaumont Park. Managed by Michelle Cassaro, ex-manager of cult lesbian club Pulp, Rosa Bonheur is an equally laidback den that embraces diversity and serves rustic food and wonderfully cheap wine. Roughly translating into "pink happiness," Rosa Bonheur is named after the 19th century feminist painter and sculptor. A retreat for hip families, students and artists, rustle up conversation with the Bonheur folk whilst grazing upon their seasonal tapas along with a glass of raspberry rosé.

🕐 1830–2345 (Tu), 1200– (W–F), 1000– (Sa–Su)
🏠 Parc des Buttes Chaumont (#9)
📞 +33 (0)1 4200 0045 URL www.rosabonheur.fr
🖉 Enter at 7 r. Botzaris when park is closed

"It's a guinguette inside of Parc des Buttes Chaumont. At night you have music and drinks with a lot of people when the weather is good."

– Violaine & Jérémy

54 New Morning
Map D, P.105

To list the musicians who have taken the stage at this music spot is to summarise the history of jazz, folk and blues. Inaugurated in 1981, talents such as Dizzy Gillespie, Chet Baker, Miles Davis and Pat Metheny have contributed to the venue's astonishing history. A premier destination for fans of avant garde world music, the auditorium boasts brilliant acoustics, having also attracted guests like Prince and Spike Lee. Located around the corner of Grands Boulevards, arrive at 8pm for a chilled drink before the concert starts at 9pm.

🕐 *2030–0000 daily*
🏠 *7–9 r. Petites Ecuries,*
Porte Saint-Denis, 75010
📞 *+33 (0)1 4523 5141*
URL *www.newmorning.com*

"*This place is historical for jazz in Paris. It's small so it's really intimate. Famous musicians play there so it can be better to book your ticket in advance.*"
– Isabelle Chapuis

55 Andy Wahloo
Map D, P.105

The neon signs, warm colours and checkered floor accompanied with pop art and hints of North African culture foreshadows the equally characteristic and fun night this gastropub will provide. Tucked away in a courtyard of restaurants all owned by the critically acclaimed Mourad Mazouz, it doesn't surprise to find a vast variety of decent alcohol and cocktails at Andy Wahloo. Their dance floor may be petite but the live DJs know how to pick out the perfect songs to match your mood.

🕐 1800–0200 (Tu-Sa)
🏠 69 r. Gravilliers, 75003
📞 +33 (0)1 4271 2038
URL andywahloo-bar.com

"Before or after a drink at Andy Wahloo, have a meal at the neighbouring restaurant Derriere (#47) located in the same courtyard."

– Flaminia Saccucci

56 **Carmen**
Map F, P.106

With its luxurious renaissance furnishings, high ceilings and hugely decadent décor, this listed building has become an unlikely haven for the capital's hipsters, creatives and fashion elite. Constructed in 1875, where Bizet wrote his famous opera, the grandiose residence and bar just south of Pigalle is a lively music spot hosting a diverse set of evenings from DJ sets and violin concerts to fashion parties and artistic performances. The ground floor is the bar area that contains numerous small chambers and even a golden cage to sit in to sip creative drinks.

🕐 1800–0600 (Tu-Sa)
🏠 34 r. Duperré,
Saint Georges, 75009
📞 +33 (0)1 4874 3310
URL www.le-carmen.fr

"Cocktails are excellent and the barman asks you what you'd like and then makes a bespoke drink for you. Be prepared to meet fancy people there!"

– Violaine d'Harcourt

57 Bus Palladium

Map F, P.106

A Parisian legend in the rock-scene, the Bus Palladium had welcomed guests like Salvador Dalí shortly after it opened its doors. Then, Mick Jagger celebrated his birthday there and the Beatles graced its stage, solidifying its status. Fifty years on, it maintains its retro style and punkness, ensuring a great time to dance all night with energetic company. Need to catch a breath or some food before heading back to the pit? Trust chef Stéfan Laugénie to fill your stomach upstairs. That's no ordinary bar food for sure.

🕐 2000–0200 (Tu–Th), –0530 (Fr–Sa)
🏠 6 r. Fontaine, Pigalle, 75009
☎ +33 (0)1 4526 8035
URL buspalladium.com

"One of the oldest clubs in Paris. Cool atmosphere!"

– Karine + Oliver

58 Le Comptoir Général
Map G, P.107

A self-styled "Ghetto museum," Le Comptoir Général is a 600sqm, two-floor venue whose mission is to showcase the creativity of marginal cultures from Africa. Encompassing a bar, greenhouse, canteen and shopping stalls, the not-for-profit stages cinema screenings, exhibitions and concerts – often centred on music, sport, religion and politics, all housed in an old hotel building in an alleyway off rue des Jemmapes. Enter through the courtyard and arrive early as queues start to form from around 8pm.

🕐 1800-0100 (M-W), -0200 (Th-F), 1600-0200 (Sa), 1100-0200 (Su)
🏠 80 quai de Jemmapes, Porte Saint-Martin, 75010
✆ contact@lecomptoirgeneral.com
🔗 www.lecomptoirgeneral.com

"It is a little bit hard to find in the first place... Go in and grab a banana-beer or just have a look at the Le Cabinet de Sorcellerie (The Cabinet of Curiosities)!"
– Wanja Ledowski, Wanja Ledowski-Studio

59 Le Non_Jazz

Providing a window into the alternative subculture that undercuts Paris street life, Le Non_Jazz is the most experimental music night in the city. Eccentric and unashamedly DIY, the night inhabits various environments each month, playing host to sonic improvisers and impulsive instrumentalists all set on pushing the boundaries of sound. Le Non_Jazz has already left a trail through trendy venues across town such as former brewery Instants Chavirés. Be sure to keep on top of their next move via their tumblr page to know where they'll next pop-up.

🕐 🏠 *Showtime & venue vary by events*
URL nnjzz.tumblr.com

"Just go! That's where you'll have a taste of Paris underground – weird, freaks and bands!"

– Mehdi Hercberg aka Shoboshobo

60 Silencio

Map D, P.104

Named after the cult venue featured in his 2001 film *Mulholland Drive*, movie director David Lynch has created an intimate private club on rue Montmartre. Descend six flights of stairs to enter the 200sqm space, a vast social hangout featuring hidden rooms, a live stage with a reflective dance floor, a small art library and a spacious 24-seat cinema, all with original furniture designed by Lynch. Concerts, film premieres and art shows are staged on a regular basis, and the club is reserved for members and their guests until midnight.

🕐 1800-0400 (Tu-Th), -0600 (F-Sa)
🏠 142 r. Montmartre, Mail, 75002
🔗 silencio-club.com
🖉 Members only before midnight

"Good music and beautiful caves... Go there to dance!"
– Alexandre Plicque-Gurlitt

DISTRICT MAPS : **GROS CAILLOU, INVALIDES, CHAILLOT, CHAMPS-ÉLYSÉES, FAUBOURG-DU-ROULE**

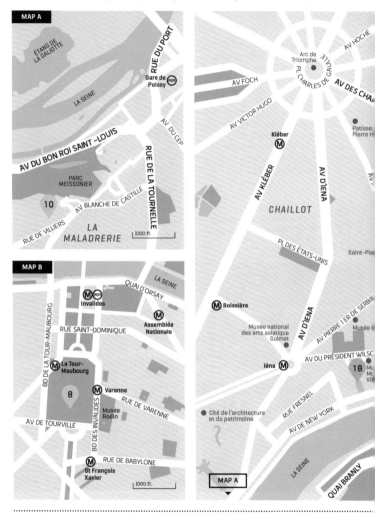

- 8_Hôtel National Des Invalides
- 10_Villa Savoye
- 18_Palais de Tokyo

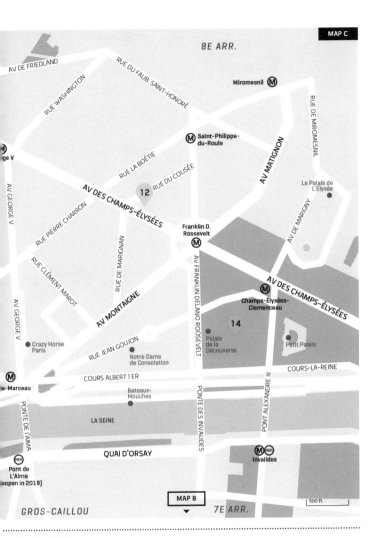

MAP C

8E ARR.

AV DE FRIEDLAND

RUE DU FAUB. SAINT-HONORÉ

Miromesnil Ⓜ

RUE WASHINGTON

RUE DE MIROMESNIL

ge V

Saint-Philippe-
du-Roule Ⓜ

AV MATIGNON

Le Palais de
L'Élysée

AV GEORGE V

RUE LA BOÉTIE

RUE DU COLISÉE

AV DES CHAMPS-ÉLYSÉES

12

RUE PIERRE CHARRON

AV DE MARIGNY

Franklin D.
Roosevelt
Ⓜ

RUE CLÉMENT MAROT

RUE DE MARIGNAN

AV FRANKLIN DELANO ROOSEVELT

AV DES CHAMPS-ÉLYSÉES

Champs-Élysées-
Clemenceau Ⓜ

AV GEORGE V

AV MONTAIGNE

14

Palais
de la
Découverte

Petit Palais

Crazy Horse
Paris

RUE JEAN GOUJON

Notre Dame
de Consolation

COURS-LA-REINE

Ⓜ
a-Marceau

COURS ALBERT 1 ER

Bateaux-
Mouches

PONTE DE L'AMA

PONTE DES INVALIDES

PONT ALEXANDRE III

LA SEINE

QUAI D'ORSAY

Ⓜ RER
Invalides

Ⓜ RER
Pont de
L'Alma
(eopen in 2018)

MAP B
▼

500 ft.

GROS-CAILLOU

7E ARR.

....

● 12_Citroën C42
● 14_Grand Palais

DISTRICT MAP : **PALAIS-ROYAL, MAIL, PLACE VENDÔME**

- 24_12 MAIL
- 30_Hôtel Drouot (Auction House)
- 38_Gioia Mia
- 42_Kunitoraya
- 60_Silencio

- 19_Backslash Gallery
- 28_THANX GOD I'M A V.I.P.
- 37_Hôtel Edgar
- 45_Café Michalak
- 47_Derrière
- 54_New Morning
- 55_Andy Wahloo

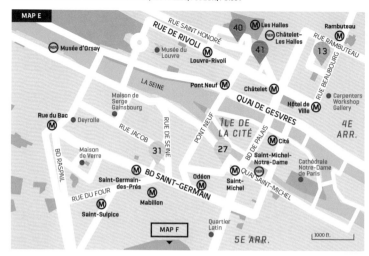

- 13_Centre Pompidou
- 15_Le Louxor
- 21_Halle Saint Pierre
- 22_Le Bal

- 27_Un Regard Moderne
- 31_Ragtime
- 33_Guerrisol
- 40_Chez Denise

- 41_Le Bistrot des Halles
- 46_ Le Bouchon des Batignolles

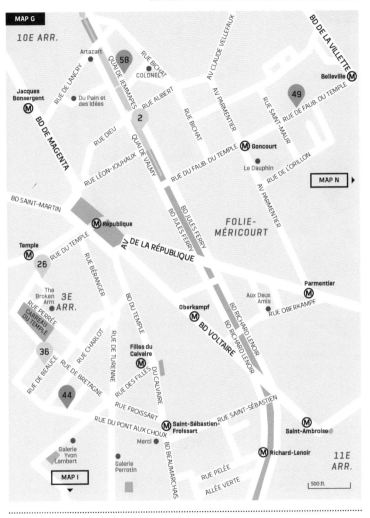

MAP G

10E ARR.

Artazart

58

RUE BICHAT

COLONEL

QUAI DE JEMMAPES

RUE DE LANCRY

Jacques
Bonsergent Ⓜ

Du Pain et
des Idées

BD DE MAGENTA

RUE ALIBERT

2

RUE DIEU

QUAI DE VALMY

RUE LÉON-JOUHAUX

BD SAINT-MARTIN

Ⓜ République

Temple Ⓜ

RUE DU TEMPLE

26

AV. DE LA RÉPUBLIQUE

RUE BÉRANGER

The
Broken
Arm

3E
ARR.

RUE PERRÉE
CARREAU
DU TEMPLE

36

RUE DE BEAUCE

RUE CHARLOT

RUE DE BRETAGNE

RUE DE TURENNE

BD DU TEMPLE

44

Galerie
Yvon
Lambert

MAP I

Galerie
Perrotin

AV CLAUDE VELLEFAUX

BD DE LA VILLETTE

RUE BICHAT

AV PARMENTIER

RUE SAINT-MAUR

Belleville Ⓜ

49

RUE DE FAUB. DU TEMPLE

RUE DU FAUB. DU TEMPLE

Ⓜ Goncourt

Le Dauphin

RUE DE L'ORILLON

MAP N ▶

AV PARMENTIER

BD JULES FERRY

FOLIE-
MÉRICOURT

Parmentier Ⓜ

Aux Deux
Amis

RUE OBERKAMPF

Oberkampf
Ⓜ

BD VOLTAIRE

BD RICHARD LENOIR

Filles du
Calvaire
Ⓜ

RUE DES FILLES
DU CALVAIRE

RUE FROISSART

RUE DU PONT AUX CHOUX

Ⓜ Saint-Sébastien-
Froissart

RUE SAINT-SÉBASTIEN

Merci

BD BEAUMARCHAIS

RUE PELÉE

ALLÉE VERTE

Ⓜ
Saint-Ambroise

Ⓜ Richard-Lenoir

11E
ARR.

500 ft.

....

◯ 2_Canal Saint-Martin	◯ 44_Chez Nénesse	◯ 56_Carmen
◯ 26_Ofr.	◯ 49_House of Moda Party	◯ 57_Bus Palladium
◯ 36_Marché des Enfants Rouges	◯ 52_Le Trianon	◯ 58_Le Comptoir Général

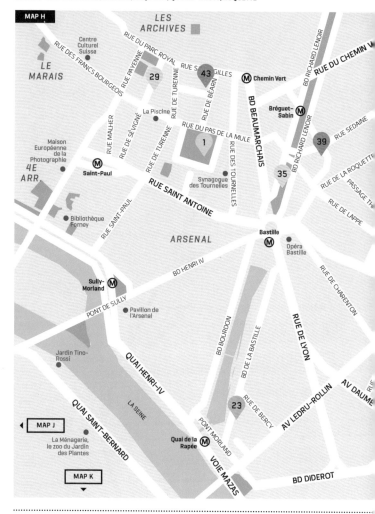

- 1_ Place des Vosges
- 23_La Maison Rouge
- 29_Comptoir de l'Image
- 35_Marché Bastille
- 39_Café de l'Industrie
- 43_Le Petit Marché

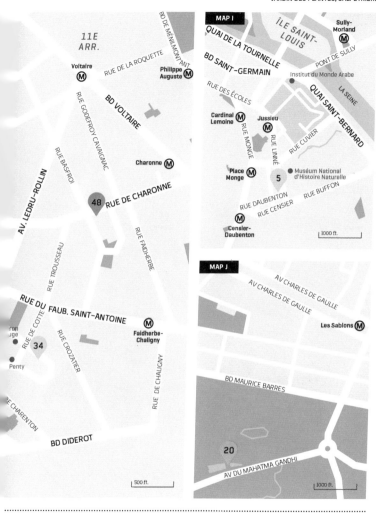

11E ARR.

MAP I

QUAI DE LA TOURNELLE

ÎLE SAINT-LOUIS

Sully-Morland

BD DE MÉNILMONTANT

RUE DE LA ROQUETTE

Voltaire Ⓜ

Philippe Auguste Ⓜ

BD SAINT-GERMAIN

PONT DE SULLY

Institut du Monde Arabe

LA SEINE

RUE GODEFROY CAVAIGNAC

BD VOLTAIRE

RUE DES ÉCOLES

QUAI SAINT-BERNARD

Cardinal Lemoine Ⓜ

Jussieu Ⓜ

RUE MONGE

RUE LINNÉ

RUE CUVIER

RUE BASFROI

Charonne Ⓜ

Place Monge Ⓜ

5

Muséum National d'Histoire Naturelle

AV. LEDRU-ROLLIN

48 RUE DE CHARONNE

RUE DAUBENTON

RUE BUFFON

RUE CENSIER

Censier-Daubenton Ⓜ

1000 ft.

RUE FAIDHERBE

RUE TROUSSEAU

MAP J

RUE DU FAUB. SAINT-ANTOINE

AV CHARLES DE GAULLE

AV CHARLES DE GAULLE

RUE DE COTTE

34

Faidherbe-Chaligny Ⓜ

Les Sablons Ⓜ

Penty

RUE CROZATIER

BD MAURICE BARRES

RUE DE CHALIGNY

RUE DE CHARENTON

20

BD DIDEROT

AV DU MAHATMA GANDHI

500 ft.

1000 ft.

- 5_Gra nde Mosquée de Paris
- 20_Fondation Louis Vuitton
- 32_FrenchTrotters
- 34_Le Marché d'Aligre
- 48_Septime

109

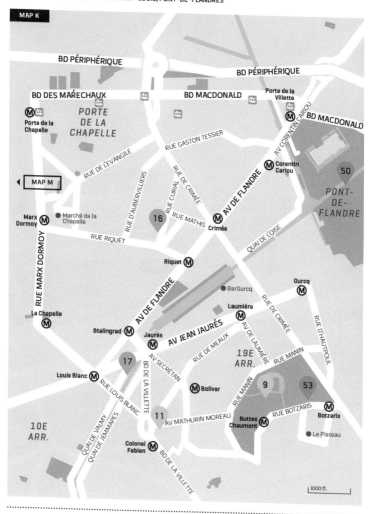

- 9_Parc des Buttes-Chaumont
- 11_Siège du PCF, Espace Niemeyer
- 16_104 Centquatre
- 17_Point Éphémère
- 50_Parc de la Villette
- 53_Rosa Bonheur

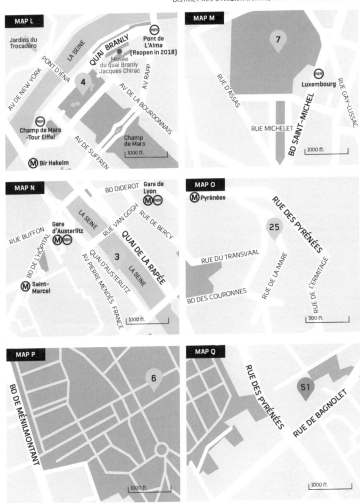

- 3_Les Docks – Cité de la mode et du design
- 4_Tour Eiffel
- 6_Cimetière du Père-Lachaise
- 7_Jardin du Luxembourg
- 25_L'Atelier Beau Travail
- 51_MAMA Shelter

Accommodation

Hip hostels, fully-equipped apartments & swanky hotels

No journey is perfect without a good night's sleep to recharge. Whether you're on vacation or a business trip, our picks combine top quality and convenience, whatever your budget.

 €81–200   *€201+*

La Maison Champs Élysées

Ease up in Maison Martin Margiela's first hotel. Located at Paris' Golden Triangle, the five-star style statement will press any fashionista's buttons with its 'Couture Collection', a streamlined union of theatrical decor and unobtrusive luxury. A real design experience. The hotel's restaurant connects the Cigar Bar, a cocktail bar and a terrace.

🏠 8 r. Jean Goujon, Champs-Élysées, 75008
📞 +33 (0)1 4074 6465
URL www.lamaisonchampselysees.com

Hôtel du Temps

With pastoral, vintage prints and natural lighting, designer Alix Thomsen creates, as in her fashion lines, moving dialogues between fabrics and touch in this Montmartre hotel. Starting at €120, 23 rooms boost home-like comfort with urban convenience. Aesop products and a light breakfast are a nice finishing touch.

 11 r. Montholon, Rouchechouart, 75009
+33 (0)1 4770 3716
URL www.hotel-du-temps.fr

Hôtel Edgar

Photographers, directors, scenographers and artists buoy up this young hotel. Its 13 rooms are imbued with 13 kinds of different passions, from childhood toys to wild African adventure, blending a charged creative energy with a charming neighbourhood vibe. The hotel's kitchen prepares upclass breakfast and meals, luring a crowd year-round.

🏠 31 r. Alexandrie, Sentier, 75002 📞 +33 (0)1 4041 0519 🔗 www.edgarparis.com

Hôtel Particulier Montmartre 💲

🏠 23, av. Junot, Montmartre, 75018
📞 +33 (0)1 5341 8140
URL hotel-particulier-montmartre.com

Hôtel Émile

🏠 2 r. Malher, Le Marais, 75004
📞 +33 (0)1 4272 7617
URL www.hotelemile.com

Notes

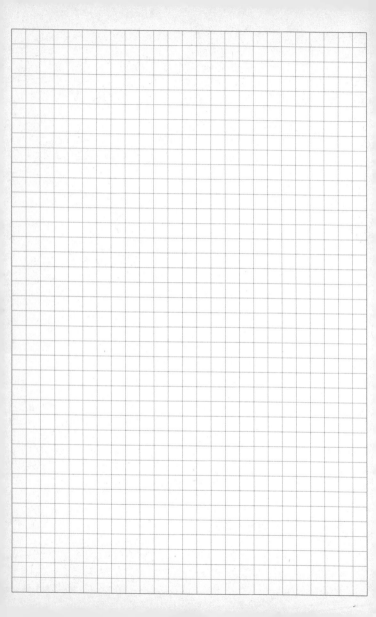

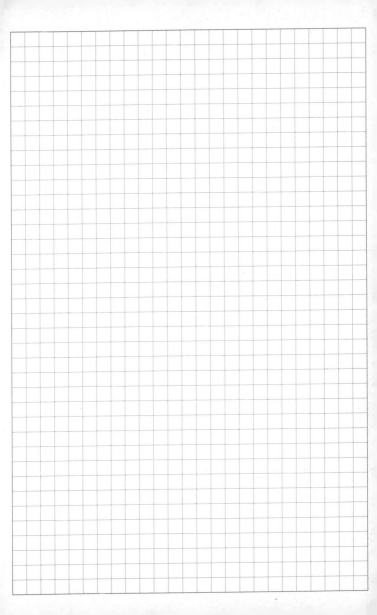

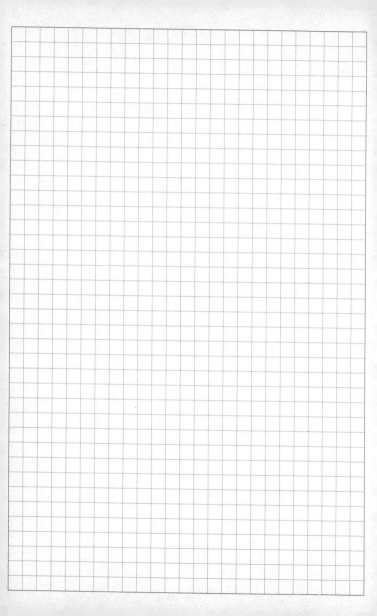

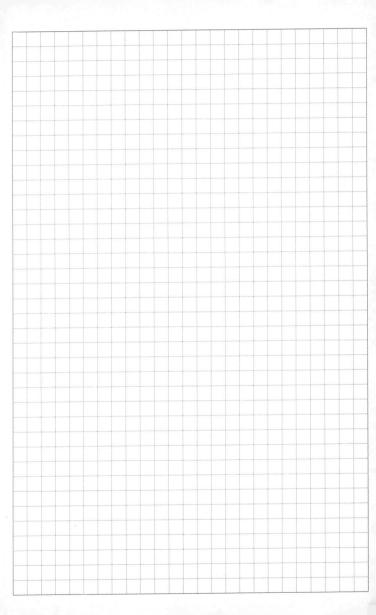

Index

Architecture

Art & Illustration

Fashion

Film

Food

Graphics

Wanja Ledowski @Wanja
Ledowski-Studio, *p098*
www.wanjaledowski.com

Industrial

ARRO Studio, *p042*
www.arro-studio.com

COLONEL, *p033*
moncolonel.fr

Patrick Norguet, *p022*
www.patricknorguet.com

Violaine d'Harcourt, *p096*
www.violainedharcourt.fr

Multimedia

Alexandre Plicque-Gurlitt,
p101
www.apg1979.com

Chic & Artistic, *p065*
chic-artistic.com

Pleix, *p078*
www.pleix.net

The Imaginers, *p081*
www.theimaginers.fr
www.man-shows.com
www.woman-shows.com

Music

Jolie Cherie, *p073*
www.facebook.com/joliecherie-
music

Leslie Dubest, *p021*
www.un-plan-simple.com

Photography

Alex VI, *p035*
www.alexvi.fr

Isabelle Chapuis, *p094*
www.isabellechapuis.com

Jean-Yves Lemoigne, *p058*
www.jeanyveslemoigne.com

Jules Faure, *p072*
julesfaure.com
www.monsieur-mademoiselle.
com

Karine + Oliver, *p097*
www.karine-oliver.com

Ruben Brulat, *p076*
www.rubenbrulat.com

Publishing

Agathe Cordelle & Olivia
Zeitline, *p038*
www.reecrire.com
www.the-editorialist.com
www.theautomart.cc

Photo & other credits

Andy Wahloo, *p097*
(All) Andy Wahloo

Carmen, *p096*
(Interior) Carmen

Fondation Louis Vuitton,
p031, 042
(All) Fondation Louis Vuitton
(Architecture) Iwan Baan
(Artwork) Middle: Gilbert &
George; Bottom: Olafur Eliasson

Gioia Mia, *p068, 071*
(p.068 & p.071 Top) Carolina
Aldrovandi *(Bottom)* Sonia
Simula @beneandada

Grand Palais, *p030, 033*
(Top) Mirco Magliocca pour la
Réunion des musées nationaux,
Grand Palais *(p.030 & p.033
Bottom)* Collection Rmn-Grand
Palais by François Tomasi

Hôtel Drouot (Auction House),
p059
(Auction room) Hôtel Drouot (Auction House)

Hôtel Edgar, *p066, 070, 114*
(All) Hôtel Edgar

La Maison Champs Élysées,
p112
(All) Martine Houghton

La Maison Rouge, *p046*
(Façade) ©Marc Domage
(Interiors) ©Luc Boegly

Bus Palladium, *p087, 095*
(p.087 & p.095 Top) Façade du
Bus Palladium, novembre 2014
by Beaugency / CC BY-SA 4.0
(Middle) Le Bus Palladium *(Bottom)* Useless Talk live at Bus Palladium in Paris by Axel Rouvin
/ CC BY 2.0

Le Comptoir Général,
p098-099
(Interiors) Le Comptoir Général

Le Louxor, *p034*
(Interiors) Le Louxor

Le Trianon, *p092*
(Top) Guillaume Guerin

MAMA Shelter, *p091*
(All) MAMA Shelter

New Morning, *p094*
(Event) Philippe Pierangeli

Silencio, *p101*
(All) ©Alexandre Guirkinger @
Silencio

THANX GOD I'M A V.I.P., *p050,
056-057*
(All) THANX GOD I'M A V.I.P.

Villa Savoye, *p013, 024*
(All) Ken Fung

In Accommodation: all courtesy
of respective hotels

CITIX60
CITIx60: Paris

Published and distributed by
viction workshop ltd

viction:ary™

7C Seabright Plaza, 9-23 Shell Street,
North Point, Hong Kong

Url: www.victionary.com
Email: we@victionary.com
🗊 @victionworkshop
🐦 @victionary_
📷 @victionworkshop

Edited and produced by viction:ary

Concept & art direction: Victor Cheung
Research & editorial: Queenie Ho, Caroline Kong
Project Coordination: Katherine Wong, Jovan Lip
Design & map illustration: Beryl Kwan, Cherie Yip

Editing: Elle Kwan
Contributing writer: Monique Todd
Cover map illustration: Allan Deas
Count to 10 illustrations: Guillaume Kashima aka Funny Fun
Photography: Matteo Mastronardi, Morphee Zhang

Content is compiled based on facts available as of December 2017. Travellers
are advised to check for updates from respective locations before your visit.

Sixth edition
ISBN 978-988-78500-1-4
Printed and bound in China

Acknowledgements

A special thank you to all creatives, photographer(s), editor, producers,
companies and organisations for your crucial contributions to our
inspiration and knowledge necessary for the creation of this book. And,
to the many whose names are not credited but have participated in the
completion of the book, we thank you for your input and continuous
support all along.

CITIX60

City Guides

CITIx60 is a handpicked list of hot spots that illustrates the spirit of the world's most exhilarating design hubs. From what you see to where you stay, this city guide series leads you to experience the best – the places that only passionate insiders know and go.

Each volume is a unique collaboration with local creatives from selected cities. Known for their accomplishments in fields as varied as advertising, architecture and graphics, fashion, industry and food, music and publishing, these locals are at the cutting edge of what's on and when. Whether it's a one-day stopover or a longer trip, **CITIx60** is your inspirational guide.

Stay tuned for new editions.

Featured cities:

Amsterdam
Barcelona
Berlin
Copenhagen
Hong Kong
Istanbul
Lisbon
London
Los Angeles
Melbourne
Milan
New York
Paris
Portland
Singapore
Stockholm
Taipei
Tokyo
Vancouver
Vienna